Deep Blue Night

The Portable Library of Korean Literature

The Portable Library of Korean Literature introduces readers around the world to the depth and breadth of a vibrant literary tradition that heretofore has been little known outside of Korea. These small books, each devoted to a single writer, will be appreciated for their originality, for their universality, and for their broad range of styles and themes. The goal of *The Portable Library of Korean Literature* is to bring Korean creative writing into the mainstream of world literature.
—Korea Literature Translation Institute

The Portable Library of Korean Literature
Short Fiction · **5**

Deep Blue Night
Choe In-ho
Translated by
Bruce and Ju-Chan Fulton

Jimoondang Publishing Company
Seoul

Deep Blue Night · The Poplar Tree
Original title: Gipgo pureun bam, Popeulla namu
© 1982&1981 Choe In-ho
© English translation 2002 Bruce and Ju-Chan Fulton
All rights reserved.

The Portable Library of Korean Literature is edited
by the Korea Literature Translation Institute.

Jimoondang Publishing Company
95 Waryong-dong, Jongno-gu, Seoul, Korea
Phone 02 743 0227, 02 743 3192-3
Fax 02 743 3097, 02 742 4657
E-mail edit@jipmoon.co.kr/ sale@jipmoon.co.kr
         jimoondang@yahoo.com
www.jimoon.co.kr

ISBN 89-88095-62-6

Printed in Korea

Book design—CHUNG DESIGN

CONTENTS

Deep Blue Night — 7

The Poplar Tree — 73

About the author — 84

About the translators — 85

Deep Blue Night

1

Awake on schedule. He flexed stiff arms, then checked his watch. Eight a.m., on the dot. No one would have awakened him. Instead, animal instinct, acutely aware of the flow of time, had roused him from a sound sleep at just the right moment, like an alarm clock.

He saw a room he didn't recognize.

Where was he? Had he fallen asleep here? Still drowsy, he searched his foggy mind for the answers. Everything was a blur—this was what the world must look like to the myopic—and his brain, despite its deathlike slumber, was a dizzying chaos, as if dust coated its every fold.

The house was quiet, but the dazzling rays of the morning sun poured in between the closed curtains.

The night before, he had arranged with Jun-ho to be awake around eight in the morning; after washing up they would leave no later than nine. But now he realized he could have slept another thirty minutes or so.

If they took Interstate 5 all the way from San Francisco, they could make it to Los Angeles in six hours. On U.S. 101, seven or eight hours would be enough. They had agreed, though, to follow Route 1 as it meandered along the coast, and there was no telling how long that would take—probably more than ten hours, driving nonstop. But even this was a wild guess, he corrected himself. Route 1 was a scenic two-lane highway constructed along a precipitous coast for much of its length, but it was closed from time to time when summer rains spawned mudslides or sent rocks tumbling from the roadside bluffs. In other words, it might require much more time. To have a good chance of reaching Los Angeles that night, they should leave around nine o'clock at the latest.

He and Jun-ho had set out from Los Angeles a week earlier on I-15. They branched off toward Death Valley on California 127 at Baker, then took 190 to Olancha and the junction with U.S. 395. This they followed south to Freeman, where they picked up 178 to Bakersfield.

Bakersfield—wasn't that the name of the protagonist of a Dickens novel? There they took Route 99 north.

At Fresno they turned onto 41, an arterial that led them to Yosemite Park. They left Yosemite on 120, and at Manteca they reencountered 99 before joining I-5, and in turn I-205, which took them to I-580 and at last to San Francisco.

They had left Los Angeles with a single road map. Following a network of roads that branched off one after another, spreading out like the strands of a spider web, they had roamed headlong among the California byways.

In a single fast swoop they had crossed deserts and snowy valleys, heading for the coast. Their plan now was to see the ocean. A look at the map was enough to tell them that Route 1, which hugged the coastline, was their best shortcut to views of the water.

The previous week had been a forced march with no letup. It had wearied them, and their only desire was to return quickly to Los Angeles. Besides, they were running out of money. They could afford another tank of gas, but even if they skimped on meals and made do with cheap hamburgers, their pockets contained barely enough for a motel room. And so today it would have to be nonstop to Los Angeles. This meant forcing themselves to leave by nine.

He struggled to a sitting position.

The cobwebs had gradually cleared from his head as he pieced together their itinerary thus far, and he was finally able to think clearly, as if his mind had found its own pair of glasses.

He'd been up drinking until two in the morning. Barely six hours of shuteye, he told himself. But it appeared he'd fallen asleep relatively early. Most likely the others had continued drinking and talking; most likely they had gotten drunker. And perhaps it was not until dawn that they had passed out in exhaustion.

Music had penetrated his deep slumber from time to time, and there had been whiffs of musty cigarette smoke, snatches of murmured conversation. He had been violently drunk when he fell asleep. Gradually succumbing to fatigue, he'd been hit all at once by the whiskey he was drinking—he must have had too much of it. And he vaguely recalled a vicious, drunken argument with someone.

He'd been ushered off to bed, and the party—a rare occasion for the host and his guests, it turned out—had likely continued until dawn.

His head was a torrent of pain. Gingerly he rose.

He opened the door and the living room met his eyes, brilliant with streams of silvery dust pouring from the morning sun.

The living room was a shambles. He saw a table strewn with whiskey bottles, glasses, the remains of overturned drinks, cigarette butts crushed out at random, records, including one that had been broken, a guitar, bread crumbs, a few bits of cheese sampled and then spit out. Also on the table was a tobacco pouch full of marijuana and a pipe and other smoking paraphernalia. The air was rank with the stink of liquor and tobacco and the harsh, scorched-grass odor of marijuana.

Half a dozen people were sprawled out on the floor, all of them oblivious in their drunken sleep to the indiscriminate assault of the sun's rays. Arms rested on legs, legs on arms. The faces were pallid like those of drowning victims hauled from the water. A woman with long hair was hugging a giant teddy bear.

He looked about for Jun-ho.

There he was, asleep on the couch, a blanket thrown over him. Judging from the bread crumbs near his head, Jun-ho had fallen asleep while eating—evidence that he'd smoked a great deal of marijuana the previous night. For Jun-ho seemed perpetually hungry when he smoked. He had once seen Jun-ho gobble a one-pound loaf of bread and three ham sandwiches after smoking.

He nudged Jun-ho's head. The other's eyes remained shut. He shook Jun-ho, a bit more forcefully. Jun-ho reluctantly opened his eyes.

"Get up," he said in a soft voice. "It's nine o'clock."

"Oh, come on," Jun-ho said, turning away. "*Hyeong*, I need more sleep—I was up till five."

He grabbed Jun-ho by the hair.

"Get up, asshole."

He noticed a woman's hairpin. It seemed one of the women had been playing with Jun-ho's hair, brushing and then fixing it in place with her hairpin. It had the shape of a butterfly and was quite lovely.

"Hey, come on—please?" Jun-ho mumbled, palms together in supplication. "Give me another hour—it's not going to matter."

"Uh-uh. We have to get going—right now."

"Will you fucking relax? This isn't Korea—it's America. Oh, all right—fuck! Where's my glasses? See them anywhere, *Hyeong*?"

He surveyed the chaos, looking for the glasses. Jun-ho had terrible eyesight. Without glasses he couldn't see his hand in front of his face. Indeed, his glasses were his eyes. He himself hadn't learned to drive, and so Jun-ho had been left with that responsibility during their journey thus far. But without his glasses Jun-ho wouldn't be able to drive.

He waded through the tangle of sleeping bodies as if foraging for household items in the ashes of a burned-down house. He stepped on someone, a man, who called out in a muffled voice, then opened his eyes and looked up.

"Sorry," he said amiably. He didn't recognize the face. He and Jun-ho had arrived at nine the previous evening after reaching San Francisco in the morning and roaming the city. They had set out for this house in San Jose around dinnertime. The only man Jun-ho knew in the area lived here. But they had only his address—no telephone number. Their pockets were almost empty, and they couldn't sleep on the streets. That left them with one choice: impose on this man's family for the night, whether he liked it or not. He had roughly sensed that Jun-ho and this man weren't close friends, but only bare acquaintances who once upon a time had happened to exchange addresses. But the nature of the relationship made no difference to Jun-ho and him. They were content to be obliged to their host for a place to sleep. A night in the garage would have suited them. All they would do was sleep and leave.

Finding the house without directions had been like snatching at clouds. They had finally arrived after nine—three hours it must have taken them. It happened to be Saturday, and half a dozen people had gathered to celebrate the weekend. Jun-ho had once been quite well known as a singer, and the other guests appeared to know this. And so the two of them had received a much warmer welcome than they'd expected. The children had been sent to the relatives, the man who lived there had informed them with a smile.

"You picked a good time," he said. "This is our first

get-together since I don't know when. Come on in and join the party."

The people inside had been drinking and their eyes had begun to glaze over. He and Jun-ho introduced themselves, shook hands, and soon were laughing along with everyone else. But now he couldn't recall a single name. He had carried on with them till two in the morning, laughing and dancing. One of the drunken women had gone swimming in the pool, clothes and all. Drunk himself, he had followed suit, he vaguely recalled; he'd jumped in wearing only his underpants. Whatever had possessed him to do that?

A five-hour stretch: from nine in the evening till two in the morning he'd talked, drank, ate, danced, and then he'd been involved in a heated argument. But now the sleeping faces were utterly unfamiliar. Who were they? What were their names? Why had he argued with them? Who was the woman who had jumped into the pool with her clothes on? As he searched the living room for Jun-ho's glasses, his mind came to a dead end. He felt as if he had run up against a rock wall.

He thought about the strange jolt he'd received at the sight of the faces appearing beneath the porch light when they had finally arrived the previous evening at the end of their tiring journey and pressed the doorbell. Those people, all of them, had looked as if they were wearing masks. They had seemed tired, exhausted, on the point of collapse, as if the end had come and their souls had just departed their bodies. They had looked like spirits of the dead, still roaming this world, souls he had janced upon while wandering a dark, desolate wilderness.

Never again could he talk with these sleeping people, never again could he see them.

This sentiment had been his constant companion during the journey, a sadness he felt when he saw a beautiful scene, a huge desert, a cactus, the grandeur of snow-covered Yosemite Park.

He couldn't see them again.

Never again could he see the scenes that had sped by at seventy miles an hour, lingering for an instant in the car window before disappearing. Encountered once, they had vanished into the eternal past. Now and then, shadows had played about on that green expanse of carpet that knew no end, on the earth shaded by the clouds. He thought back to his childhood: When we were kids we used to throw shadows on the wall with our hands under the dim lantern light of our room in the evening. We'd bend our fingers and make foxes, rabbits, dogs.

Pesky clouds had concealed the sun from time to time, draping the earth with shadow. Sometimes the clouds would bring a sprinkle, sometimes before vanishing they would seem to gently caress the earth, as if combing tousled hair. A playful sprinkle from a fleeting cloud, a moment's gloom casting cool shadow everywhere as if to relieve boredom—never again could he see them.

Those clouds, that sunlight, the shiny baldpate clouds above distant plains, the occasional spindly trees resembling sparse pubic growth—he couldn't see them again.

Never again could he see the route they had taken— Interstate 5, U.S. 101, Death Valley, the desert, Bakersfield. Or the faces of these sleeping people whose names he couldn't remember. He would never be able to recall their voices, their laughter, and they for their part would soon forget for all time this single chance encounter.

He found Jun-ho's glasses next to a stereo speaker. They looked like they'd been stepped on—the frame was badly bent—but the lenses, thank heaven, were intact. He returned to Jun-ho, who had fallen sound asleep again while he'd wasted time hunting for the glasses. He roughly prodded Jun-ho's head. Moaning, Jun-ho opened his eyes.

He fitted the glasses on Jun-ho's face.

"Get up—it's nine-thirty."

Jun-ho groaned, then sat up, yawning.

"Where'd you get all that energy? Dammit, *Hyeong*,

you went to bed early. It was after five by the time I got to sleep."

"Let's move—once we're out of here you'll be wide awake. We're just wasting time here."

"Oh fuck!" Jun-ho laughed. "You're acting like someone who has to spend the night out and now he wants to go home. This is America, *Hyeong*. And you think they're going to have a brass band waiting for us in Los Angeles? You think Los Angeles is Seoul? Shit! My head's killing me. Where's the coffee?"

Just then something red and watery began to dribble from Jun-ho's nose.

"Now what! I'm bleeding." Jun-ho took a Kleenex, crumpled it into a ball, stuffed it up his nostril. Then he rose. "Socks must be around here somewhere."

Jun-ho fumbled beneath the sofa. He located one sock, then found its mate near the head of a woman who was sound asleep. Groaning, Jun-ho put on the socks, then stared at the woman's face.

"*Hyeong*—what's this lady's name?"

"Beats me. I was really plastered last night."

"That you were," Jun-ho giggled. "Loon drunk. If these folks woke up now, there's a good chance they'd gang up and kill you. *Hyeong*—you went overboard last night. I mean, jumping in the pool and all. And you know who broke that record? You, *Hyeong*."

Jun-ho gave a cheerful laugh.

"And that broken window there—you picked up a rock beside the pool and wheeee! Good thing we stopped you, or you would have wrecked the house. God, it was funny—you were so crazy. And then you got really wild and said you were going to burn down the house."

He began to feel ashamed of himself. "Well, we'd better hurry, then—before they wake up."

"You could piss on their faces and it wouldn't matter," said Jun-ho. "Dancing, smoking dope, boozing it up all night—they play awful hard, these folks."

Once the bleeding was under control, Jun-ho extracted the wad of tissue paper from his nostril and left it in an ashtray.

"All right," Jun-ho said. "Let's go—shit."

He forded the mass of sleeping bodies. Jun-ho, meanwhile, opened the refrigerator and stuffed a plastic bag with milk, bread, and cans of juice.

"Coffee, coffee, clear my head. Yeah—where's the coffee?..."

Off to the side of the living room a man was sleeping, his nose buried in the floor. Jun-ho shook him.

"Hey, friend. Hey."

The man scowled, mumbled something, then opened his eyes.

"Hey, friend, we're leaving. Thanks. Hey, friend?—Hang on. *Hyeong*, what's our pal here's name? And the man who lives here?"

"Don't recall."

"Wait a minute.... I wrote his name down—it's around here somewhere."

Jun-ho emptied his pockets. But the scrap of paper in question seemed to have taken flight.

"Hey, friend!"

But the man's eyes, which he had opened with such effort, were closed again.

Jun-ho patted the man's face. "We're leaving!" he yelled. "Thanks, friend! If you're ever in Los Angeles, get in touch!"

"So long," the man mumbled in a sleepy voice.

"Much obliged to you for putting us up," Jun-ho said softly. "We're going."

"Take care. Take..."

Jun-ho picked up the bag of edibles and called out spiritedly: "Let's go, *Hyeong*!"

They stepped outside and the rude brilliance of the sunshine exploded in their faces like a thousand camera flashes. There in front of the house the sunlight appearing so suddenly and the dark green foliage, the roses, the groves of trees—all that they had missed, arriving in the dark—roared down at them. The twittering of a flock of birds that had settled on the lawn tickled their ears.

If not for the familiar black car parked beside the garden in front of the house, the unexpected sight of that garden would have disoriented them. The car resembled a rusty old ship moored along the shore. Rain, snow, dust, and mud had left it filthy after its constant journey of a thousand-plus miles. The dust-covered windows were a translucent gray save for the fan-shaped semicircles cleared by the windshield wipers. Had they really driven this old claptrap virtually nonstop for a week? Jun-ho had paid a Mexican two thousand dollars for the unsightly thing, and to their surprise it had held out, a faithful slave suffering its small agonies in silence. Except for overheating on the steep road through Death Valley, it had run its merry way in perfect health for the entire trip.

They climbed inside. The interior was a mess: cigarette butts; bread crumbs; wornout clothes; photos of nude women clipped from a *Penthouse* magazine; the tire chains they'd bought in Yosemite Park; a road atlas, dog-eared after only a week's use, with a detailed map of California. But now that they were actually sitting in the car they began to swell with a queer sense of happiness and relief.

And now, to leave.

"Wait a minute." Jun-ho released the steering wheel

and turned to him. "That would have been a big mistake, *Hyeong*. I'll be right back."

Jun-ho got out, walked around the garden, and disappeared inside the house.

He found the pack of cigarettes that had fallen under the seat and lit one. The inside of his mouth was sandy and he couldn't taste the cigarette. More searching beneath the seat yielded the scrap of paper with the address they had sought the previous evening as if it were their only hope of salvation. He retrieved the paper.

"Jeong Jun-hyeok."

The name of the man whose house they had just slept at. A name at once familiar yet unfamiliar. The name of someone he'd never see again. Once he and Jun-ho left, the fact that this house existed on the face of the earth would be buried forever in oblivion. Once they left, there would surely be no trace in their memories of this house where they'd spent a night. And so it had been with Yosemite. They'd slept at a cabin there, and the next morning they'd exclaimed in astonishment at the upright trunks of the mammoth firs standing guard nearby, at the sun gleaming on the mountains beyond the groves of snow-covered trees. Frozen waterfalls streamed down from the summits, like the lines inscribed in one's palm. The snowy summits were pale towers looming skeletal in the winter sky, whose blue had paled almost to nothingness. We left Yosemite and came here, he told himself, and when we leave here, the memories of Yosemite will grow hazy in the recesses of our jumbled minds, some forgotten at once, some lodging like fishbones and recurring. But this house itself would continue to exist after they left—just like the evergreens would remain for all time after they left snowy Yosemite Valley. After they left Route 180, that road would always remain. Fresno would always remain, as would San Francisco. It's like when we read a thick book: we scour it with our eyes and transfer the contents to our memory while summarily dismissing the pages. Just as we don't read a book backwards, we couldn't retrace the route we took here and find it exactly as it was before.

Jun-ho appeared from the house with his pipe and the tobacco pouch full of marijuana.

Of course, he thought—no way Jun-ho would leave *that* behind.

"*Hyeong*, that would have been a disaster." With a contented smile Jun-ho eased himself behind the wheel. "This is terrific stuff. Very expensive, too. More than sixty dollars for what's in this pouch, I'll bet."

Ever so carefully Jun-ho placed the two articles in the glove compartment.

"Throw this away like you did last time and I'll bust

your head—I don't care who you are. Got it?"

"Got it."

Jun-ho produced the ignition key, put it in the switch, and gave a twist. The engine purred to life.

"Beautiful, isn't it? This baby is one class act."

Spirits up, Jun-ho pounded on the steering wheel. The horn accidentally blared a couple of times. The flock of birds on the lawn rose all together, numerous pairs of clapping hands.

"All right, let's go," said Jun-ho. "We're off. So long, scumbag house. So long, idiot sons and daughters of bitches."

Jun-ho put the car in reverse, and then they were off. He glanced back at the house. The light gray dwelling was a gleam that rose momentarily from the bluish green trees and then died out. He tried to graft a strong impression of that scene upon his mind, pulled again by the current in which he had been caught ever since the beginning of this journey. It was just like having to underscore with a red pencil every paragraph that impressed you in a book. Sure, it was a bother, but then the next time, you could skim the book, flipping through the pages, and the striking passages would appear before your eyes. Someday, long after this journey was over and he was back home, he'd have to marshal his powers of concentration if he were to recall the scenes, the numerous memories inscribed in his mind. He was like someone who gets lost and then regains his bearings by observing the position of the stars or the pattern of growth rings in a stump.

But the car was already speeding along furiously, and before the house could imprint itself on his memory it grew indistinct in the distance. All that remained, it seemed to him, was an obligation to forget it. And that's what he decided to do.

2

The weather was fine, unbelievably fine. California weather, best in the United States. It was winter, but still the gentle sunshine breathed ripeness into the tangerines, the oranges, the abundant produce of the state. That sunshine was like a flour of tiny corpuscles. It held no moisture, would crinkle and disintegrate if you seized it. It seemed to issue even from the shade, from above the fruit of the coconut trees. The shade was as dense as the sunshine was dazzling, but contained pockets of gilded powder glittering like fish scales.

San Jose was behind them now. To arrive at Route 1 they had to go by way of 101. By leaving this road at Salinas they could reach the coast.

His job was to read the map; the driving was left to Jun-ho. And so it had been throughout the previous week's journey. A mile or two from their exit, a road sign loomed overhead. Look away for an instant and you'd miss the interchange, and in turn your sense of direction. And once you lost your direction while roaring down an expressway, getting back on track was every bit as annoying as having to unbutton a jacket you'd buttoned up wrong and then do it up correctly.

Everything rolled by at a frenzied pace, giving the illusion that the expressway itself and not the car was moving along at a frightening speed. You felt you were sitting still as you held the wheel. The expressway scampered along madly; the coconut trees scudded alongside, looming tall like seven-foot basketball players. The speeding vehicles were driving toward the basket, with the trees poised to block the shot. You felt trapped on a huge escalator. At such a furious pace, if you didn't keep your eyes on the road you'd miss the junction sign, and once you lost your bearings you were nothing more than a crude reject from an automaton that assembled, sectioned, and packaged.

The expressway was a huge conveyor belt, the vehicles rolling along it quickly manufactured goods. For Jun-ho the driver, holding fast to the course, and him, ever mindful of the surroundings, controlling this frightening mechanism was like avoiding defeat in a murderous war. The map was their sole compass.

"*Hyeong*, what's going on? We should've seen the sign by now!" barked Jun-ho. He'd been racing the car along for half an hour since leaving San Jose on 101. "Fuck! You got to keep your eyes open. Salinas!"

He fixed Jun-ho with a bloodshot glare. "I know that!" he shouted back. "I've been looking out for it all along!"

Morgan Hill...Gilroy...and then Prunedale, where California 156 branched off. They'd just now passed through Prunedale. Next came Santa Rita. Once past Santa Rita, they'd reach Salinas and signs for the turnoff to Route 1.

"Salinas, Salinas," he muttered, so as not to forget. Salinas—what did the name mean? It was just a small city along a highway between San Francisco and Los Angeles. American cities? Except for their size they were all alike. Same buildings, same expressways, same supermarkets, hamburger joints with identical names, mammoth chain stores. The same faces, the same language, the same culture. The cities were inevitably the domain of the darkies, their downtowns a jumbled mess of grafitti and litter.

He rather hoped there was something different about this approaching city of Salinas, though he'd been betrayed thus far in such expectations.

"Salinas, Salinas." He mimicked the voice of a

conductor announcing intermediate stops on a train. "The next stop is Salinas. Would those passengers bound for Salinas please prepare to exit the coach?"

Salinas. S-A-L-I-N-A-S. Salinas.

What would he find there? Dinosaurs? The skull of some undiscovered anthropoid, buried beneath the steps of a hamburger joint? A poison-tipped arrowhead that had slain a paleface rushing westward for gold, buried in someone's yard? Salinas, Salinas, a name he'd often heard. Right, it was the setting for John Steinbeck's *East of Eden*—hadn't that joker compared Salinas to the Garden of Eden?

He'd traveled thousands of miles in America by now, and at mealtime he ate at the indistinguishable fast-food restaurants you could see in any city. Same construction, same prices, same appearance, same menu. Eating a hot dog or ice cream, he saw the city's youth absorbed in slaying alien space invaders in the video games flashing in the corner.

Only when eating was he likely to stop in one of those cities. But to those young people, it was the city where they'd been born and raised, where hair had sprouted in their crotches in due course, where they'd courted, married, grown old. Some would die there. Others would leave. Perhaps the unlucky ones were already dead, casualties of the Korean War or the jungles of

Vietnam—their entire lives representing to him no more than thirty minutes. While he ate pastries or ice cream they were living out their lives there. And when he finished eating and left the unfamiliar restaurant, the unfamiliar city, they would meet their deaths.

Salinas.

What could he find there? The same old act—birth, growth, young people standing in the corner of the same kind of restaurant slaying harmless aliens; love, childbearing, death.

A thunderous shout brought him to his senses: "What are you doing! We're in Salinas! What's the deal?... You're acting kind of weird, *Hyeong*. Off in another world. Crazy. Fuck! What are we supposed to do now? Wake up!"

Jun-ho's voice was exasperated. His eyes kept darting to the rear-view mirror as he flicked on his turn signal to change lanes.

The last sign for Route 1 appeared on an overpass. Exit signs always appeared three or four exits early. They told you the next three exits, and with each successive sign the road number initially appearing at the bottom would work its way to the top. This was how you knew the road you wanted was approaching.

And so they'd almost missed the turnoff to Route 1. Jun-ho turned to him with a look not quite of relief.

"I'll bet you're hungry—well, help yourself to some bread. What's the matter with you—can't even give me directions."

He didn't respond. And he wasn't hungry.

The car skirted Salinas on an expressway. No anthropoid skull remained there, no Indian arrowhead. Only the same coconut trees, the same houses, the same streets, appearing on both sides of the expressway.

Now all they had to do was follow Route 1 down the coast. Jun-ho, perhaps feeling a certain sense of security, turned on the radio. Jun-ho had a bad habit: he liked his music very loud. He'd rigged the car with his own amplifier so he could listen at top volume. The idea was not so much to enjoy the music as to shower himself with it.

With the windows rolled up tight, he himself felt trapped in a closet. In this small, speeding closet the piercing sound of the music was torture. But he made up his mind not to reveal these feelings.

Jun-ho had been two years behind him in high school. His own brother was the same age as Jun-ho and fast friends with him, and so he himself felt more than the usual intimacy between fellow alumni. Encountering Jun-ho in Los Angeles had been sheer coincidence.

He'd left Korea to travel, as had Jun-ho, but their objectives differed. Jun-ho had decided that traveling here presented an opportunity, that he should seize that opportunity and sink roots. For a time Jun-ho had enjoyed quite a reputation as a singer, and he himself had written the words to several of Jun-ho's songs. But Jun-ho had an unlucky past: at the height of his popularity he'd been barred from the stage for the "crime" of smoking marijuana. In the four years since, he'd tried his hand at one thing or another and managed to accumulate a fair amount of money, but eventually had squandered it all away. He'd written commercial jingles, he'd managed a men's apparel shop, somewhat later he'd run a tangerine farm on Jeju Island. But his wanderlust had left him with empty pockets. In the end, even after the pardon for the "marijuana singers" was announced, he didn't resume singing. He realized he was past his prime, and his voice had never been that good anyway. He was married with two children, but when the opportunity to travel to America came his way he decided to make use of it. And so he'd made his way overseas, and his visa had expired. Now that he was here, Jun-ho had told him, he would sink roots.

He had asked Jun-ho why he wasn't returning.

"Because it scares me there. Like when you wake up from a bad dream. Fuck that! I'm staying here."

He'd tried to convince himself that Jun-ho's past had made him that way, a bitter past that had forced him to live the last four years as a vagabond. He knew all too well. Including Jun-ho, many young singers had been rounded up as drug addicts and beaten, had been committed to mental hospitals, in the end had been ostracized by society for moral depravity, then shunned. A bitter past. If they'd been treated as lawbreakers, they could have gotten off with a year's probation. But instead they'd been ostracized—buffeted by public opinion and gagged indefinitely by a peculiar oppression. This must have been the motive for Jun-ho's slide from an accidental tourist to a stowaway in America.

Jun-ho was flat broke. He'd exhausted most of his travel money and the rest had gone for the car. Two months in Los Angeles was enough to make him feel keenly the need for a car; without one he couldn't budge from the city. Originally he'd arrived in New York, and from there he'd gone to Chicago, then stolen into Los Angeles. There he'd been living in a downtown boarding house that looked like something out of a nightmare—a place where a hundred dollars a month bought you a room. This huge Victorian mansion had once been a magnificent residence, but due to its slum location it had grown filthy, dilapidated, shabby—just another large dwelling.

It was then that he'd encountered Jun-ho, who was idling away the days in that rented room. Jun-ho's tourist visa had expired, and in a few days so would the first extension on it. Over time the friends who at first had welcomed Jun-ho began to keep him at a respectful distance, and the moment he embraced his plan to settle in America and try to survive here, they tried to prevent him, and then they ridiculed him, and finally they gave him the cold shoulder. Jun-ho was well aware that for lack of a convincing reason he couldn't extend his visa again.

It had been more than half a year since Jun-ho had left Korea, and although he'd been adapting reasonably well to American life, he wasn't really a tourist and wasn't really a legal immigrant, but a stranger who was somewhere in between. Jun-ho had put in a telephone—you could do that here for only twenty dollars—but all he used it for was to make collect calls, night or day, across the Pacific. During the several days he himself had stayed in Jun-ho's fleabag room, sharing a bed with him, Jun-ho's shouts in the course of these calls he made at all hours had penetrated his sleep.

"It's me.... What are you up to?... I'm in America—Los Angeles.... How's life over there? Is it snowing?... That much? Must have fouled up traffic, huh?... No snow here—it's summer year around.... Anything exciting going on?... You sound like you got a cold or something. Better make sure you and the little woman are all tucked in at night.... Hey, man, how many gigs a day you got going, anyway?... Well, don't run yourself into the ground.... Do you get to see my wife now and then?... Why don't you give her a call once in a while, buy her a meal. But don't get any ideas, scumbag."

Jun-ho's address book was crammed with the phone numbers of everyone he knew—friends, contacts at broadcasting stations, people he used to work with, old girlfriends. In the course of a night he'd place several collect calls to Korea, too foolish to realize that the more he made these calls the less welcome they were. Obtusely he continued calling, seemingly unaware that the same people who unfailingly accepted the first couple of calls would now refuse them, having discovered how expensive they were.

He himself knew. He knew that Jun-ho would finally be unable to call anyone, to communicate with anyone by phone. Jun-ho had wasted a healthy amount of his remaining money on marijuana. But in spite of his bitter experience with this weed over the past four years, he'd continued to spend unsparingly on it, exhausting his hard-earned money, poisoning himself on it day and night. Marijuana was everything to him—he would rather smoke it than eat. Marijuana was his sustenance, his booze, his water, his lifeblood. He smoked it first thing in the morning, he smoked it even while driving.

It was widely rumored among the Korean community in Los Angeles that Jun-ho was smoking again. And so people began to give up on him. "Shameless son of a bitch," they called him. He was the last person you'd look to for moral guidance. He was human trash—a guy who scrounged money from his friends to buy marijuana. What this meant was that after just three months in Los Angeles he was becoming an inveterate panhandler. No one sought him out. He was like someone who had decided to die a lingering death by taking a tiny dose of poison with his daily food and drink.

And then he and Jun-ho had run into each other.

"*Hyeong*, this is great! Let's you and me stick around here and live together."

He himself had no better idea to offer.

Jun-ho had no concrete plans, no options as to what they would do, or what his family would do if he continued to live in his present manner.

"Fuck it. We'll send the kids to an orphanage and the wife can find herself a sugar daddy. I'll see 'em one of these days. Fuck it." This was how he talked when he was high on marijuana, giggling, eyes glazed.

From the time he'd left on this trip with Jun-ho, he'd decided he would try his best to put his own mind at ease. When two people traveled together, even best friends, it was inevitable that the shortcomings of each would be magnified in the eyes of the other. And so even trivial incidents gave rise to raised voices, arguments, animosity, and violence.

They'd had one blowup already, at the entrance to Yosemite Park. It stood to reason that Yosemite, being well above sea level, would be snow-covered in winter. And yet they didn't have chains for the car. It was only natural, then, that the ranger at the park entrance turned them away. Fifty dollars they had never expected to spend—and for them a huge sum—went for a set of chains. They had no other choice. And neither of them had ever put chains on a tire. The old man who ran the gas station where the chains were sold offered to install them for thirty dollars. Thirty dollars? It was absurd. And so they did it themselves, after a desperate struggle in the snowy back lot of the station. By then a blizzard had reduced visibility almost to nothing.

They'd worked out a plan: he would make sure the chains were spread out evenly while Jun-ho turned the wheels one revolution. But something went wrong. The car lurched forward and the hand holding the chains was very nearly crushed.

"Watch it!" he snarled. "You almost ran over my hand!"

He'd snatched his hand away only to cut it on the sharp metal edge of the chassis. He peered at the bleeding hand as it stiffened in the snowy cold.

"Now what did you do that for?!" Jun-ho barked from the driver's seat. "Fuck—we almost had it on!"

He thrust his bloody hand at Jun-ho. "And *you* almost crushed my hand, you idiot! Do you understand? My hand was under the wheel and you came *this* close to running over it!"

Jun-ho slapped the hand aside. "What are you so scared of? It's not as if you broke it or something!"

An uncontrollable, murderous hatred came over him. He snatched up the remaining chain. "Out of the car, asshole!"

"Hey, those chains are for the wheels, not my face," Jun-ho mumbled with a grin, trying to calm him.

He grabbed Jun-ho by the hair and bounced him as hard as he could against the seatback. To his surprise, Jun-ho didn't resist. Suddenly he felt ashamed of himself—Jun-ho was so meek, shunning violence. He despised himself for overreacting, felt like spitting in his own face, or worse. At the same time, he didn't feel like apologizing just then. In any event, the two of them now shared a common destiny, and this realization, however depressing, settled over him as his rage cooled.

If he'd taken the chains to Jun-ho's skull, then what? How would they get across those snow-draped mountains? It wasn't Jun-ho's fault, that simmering rage and hostility he himself had felt from the very beginning.

Ever since he'd left Kimpo Airport in the autumn that rage—a desperate, pent-up anger—had been seething, waiting to erupt. In that sense he wasn't leaving on a journey. Rather he felt he was trying to escape something. All along—at Disneyland, at Universal Studios, in Hollywood, at the Korean restaurants, in the cheap apartment of a Hollywood prostitute, even while pressing his lips to the golden hair of her crotch—he felt the crimson tongue of that rage licking, ever licking at him.

It wasn't the chains that had made him lose his temper. It wasn't Jun-ho's uncivil tongue that had incited him to fury. Rather, everything angered him—what he saw, heard, said, felt—everything. He'd been angry from the moment he'd left Kimpo—angered by the eyes of his wife, who was sending him off; angered by the bracken-fern hands of his two children; angered by the fingertips of the customs official inspecting his baggage in Los Angeles. Not long before, he'd struck his wife at the height of an argument—it was the first time. "You've changed, honey," she had sobbed. "You're acting so strange." He'd been angered by the novel he was serializing in the newspaper, angered by every story or novel he'd written. He was angered by the sight of his sentences in print, by the sight of the newspaper that carried them. The screws of the self-restraint that might have checked that anger loosened, and he was powerless before the rage that gushed out. Crouching before a theater showing a movie version of one of his novels, he had clenched his teeth like some wounded beast that would never heal.

This rage had begun to alarm him. He had written it off as exhaustion. Fearing another nervous breakdown, he'd tried to psychoanalyze himself. Never in the previous ten years had he enjoyed a moment's rest, and because of overwork it seemed his nerves, like overwound violin strings, had snapped—or so he tried to rationalize it. But he could no longer check or suppress this unbearable hatred. It leaped from his mouth; like an involuntary muscle, it set his fingers in motion. At a drinking party, liquor would set him to arguing with whoever happened to be sitting across from him, and there were times when he smashed bottles and overturned tables. Leaving Korea to travel had been an escape from a life completely colored by rage.

Arriving late at night at the Los Angeles airport and walking down a long corridor, he wondered if he wasn't so much a runaway as an exile. Yes, this wasn't a journey; it wasn't an escape from day after day of an inexplicable, surging rage, but rather a departure on a road to exile. But he wasn't a political exile, for he wasn't a politician. He hadn't fled his country for the sake of artistic freedom, for he wasn't a musician. If he had dared to compare himself to such people, he would have been revealed as no more than your everyday intellectual. Once he'd interviewed Vladimir Ashkenazi after the latter's defection to the West for the sake of freedom of musical expression. When he asked why Ashkenazi had abandoned his Soviet fatherland, here is what the pianist had to say: "To be free to sit at the piano anytime I want to play. And, to be free to rest anytime I don't want to play."

But why am I exiling myself? he had wondered upon arriving in Los Angeles. Is it more freedom I want? Banishment from my anger? Banishment from a stifling everyday life?

"Remember what you did last night?"

Immersed in the ear-splitting music pouring from the speakers, Jun-ho had turned to him with a dreamy smile that suggested equal parts enjoyment of the music and absorption in driving.

They'd left the eight-lane expressway for a four-lane highway, and so the road was that much narrower. The ocean was still nowhere to be seen. Their car was speeding toward the Monterey Coast.

"You were out of your mind, *Hyeong*."

"Turn that down a bit." He spoke curtly, trying as best he could to conceal his emotions.

Jun-ho lowered the volume.

"Those folks must be awake by now. Who knows, maybe they're out looking for you. 'Cause you were off your rocker, *Hyeong*—all the way."

"Beats me—I don't remember a thing."

"Well, you polished off half a bottle of whiskey. You were okay to begin with. You said hello to everybody, shook hands, did some dancing. So far so good. But then you started to lose it. And those scumbags started picking arguments with you—'We're U.S. citizens. Korea isn't our country anymore.' And that's when you got violent. What is it with you? *Hyeong* the patriot? What a riot. I never realized you were such a patriot. And the way you were shouting: 'Watch what you're saying, assholes! Where do you sons of bitches get off talking like that!' Remember? *Big* mistake, *Hyeong*. What gives? You're the big nationalist, huh? Smashing records, breaking windows. If we hadn't done something, you would have smashed every window in the house. You don't remember that?"

"No." His tone was dismal.

It was a lie. Like stumps of trees revealed here and there through thick morning fog, fragments of the previous night floated hazily in his memory like solitary islands.

"I've never seen anyone blow up like that. You were

like somebody in a gangster movie. Just plain out of your mind."

So, he had finally exploded. Arms folded, keeping his silence, he thought about it. His latent rage had shot forth like a bullet. The whiskey, combined with his extreme fatigue, must have triggered his suppressed anger.

"They weren't trying to get you exercised over a political discussion—they were just trying to have some fun and they started talking politics. That can be fun, you know. Just like when Koreans get together they talk about which actresses were at that party where Park Chung Hee was shot—same old topic of conversation, but they're just having fun. It was nothing intentional. You overreacted, *Hyeong*. We should be thankful to those folks. They put us up for the night, we ate there, we drank there. And what do we do? We make off with juice, bread, milk, dope, when we leave. I don't know who they are, or anything—just some people I ran into at a Korean restaurant in L.A. They told me to stop by if I was up San Francisco way and they gave me their address. That's all. And you go and ruin their party.— Hey, the ocean! Look at that! The ocean! The great Pacific!"

Jun-ho honked the horn.

He stuck his head out the window to look. Beyond the

hill leading down to the resort area of Monterey was the sea.

A great many yachts and other boats were moored along the shore. The breeze carried a rich saltwater smell. Sunbathers from neighboring towns and cities could be seen, their cars parked near the marinas. This was not yet the boundless ocean of their imagination. Seagulls rode the wind like kites, soaring above sails and masts. An elderly gentleman was feeding the gulls on a jetty. The birds clustered about him in dark, thick flocks.

The gulls seemed accustomed to humans. They perched confidently on the man's head, on the palms of his hands, their sharp beaks spearing his offerings. The ocean came right up to the city here, calm and still, like a huge lake. The midday sunshine dazzled the eye, like oil dancing in a frypan.

"Monterey—famous summer resort. Rich folks from all over the world live here."

Trees and shrubs grew in lush profusion along the road. Expensive homes towered like castles above groves of windbreaks that resembled folding screens. Among the groves were verdant lawns surrounded by masses of people. *Must be a golf course.* There, a leisurely entourage—a tournament in progress?

"You know, the ocean you see in movies? It's all filmed here. Look at those houses. What the hell kind of people do you suppose live in places like that? Look how huge they are—it's ridiculous!... Want to take a look around? Monterey's supposed to be famous for tourists."

Jun-ho chattered incessantly in great excitement.

He himself, though, wasn't interested in the least. He'd been told Los Angeles bristled with high-class dwellings for the affluent, and for that one reason he had inspected Beverly Hills, which was quilted with such homes. There he found, true to these reports, magnificent mansions sprawling among groves of tropical vegetation run rampant. They weren't so much homes as castles.

"I'm going to live in a house like that, *Hyeong*. Have me a white man for a butler, and a servant like that fat black woman in *Gone With the Wind*. Don't be surprised. Koreans live in some of those houses—that's what I heard. They've socked away millions of dollars over here—used to be higher-ups in the government, keeping a low profile now, right over there. They have their own security people. Ridiculous sons of bitches. Got rich on our taxes and then ran off over here. *Hyeong*. Suppose I sold off everything back in Korea—how much you think I could raise? There's the apartment—that ought to be good for a hundred thousand dollars. And then the Jeju tangerine farm—what do you think, fifty thousand? A hundred thousand? And all my furniture, the TV, fridge, stereo—think I could get fifty thousand for all that stuff? So we're talking about two hundred fifty thousand. Not bad, huh? Guess what, *Hyeong*—I'm a rich man too! Not too many guys in America with a quarter million in cash."

All of this, he himself knew very well, was so much hot air. Jun-ho possessed only a small apartment, and that barely. And hadn't Jun-ho himself said he'd long since turned over control of the tangerine farm to others after the business had failed? This was merely a childish game Jun-ho enjoyed, a product of his willful imagination and inflated dreams. He was like a child building sand castles.

He himself had been immune to surprises, had felt no emotion—not at the Beverly Hills mansions, not at the elaborate cartoon characters at Disneyland, or the Haunted Mansion, not at the barren expanse of Death Valley, at after-dark Las Vegas, the city of never-night, or at the snow-draped Yosemite landscape.

His problem had been a thoroughgoing, pathological lack of feeling. "Big"—his only reaction to what he had seen. He hadn't taken this journey out of curiosity.

He hadn't taken it to see Beverly Hills, to see *Deep Throat* in Hollywood, to see the toy soldiers at Disneyland.

The sole purpose of his journey was *not* to see. He was no different from a blind man.

His journey to America was a journey to a self-chosen land of exile. America's opulent civilization and magnificent landscapes didn't intimidate him in the least, prompted no feelings of inferiority. He was nothing but an offender from a tiny island who'd been banished to the continent.

To those on the continent, the island where he was born and raised, where he'd loved and coupled, where he'd married and bore children, where he would age and die, amounted to no more than a tiny hamlet.

An island of wretched, foolish aboriginal people where neighbors fought over a piece of fruit from an overhanging tree, where war broke out over a stream passing through a village. That he could style himself an intellectual was a matter at best of knowing that a chicken had two legs whereas a dog had four. Being an intellectual, a person who could count from one to ten, he knew of course that the sun rose in the east and set in the west. He believed that his function as an intellectual was only to teach all he knew to the aboriginal people.

And so he taught the aboriginals six, seven, and eight, for they couldn't count beyond five, and one day all the knowledge at his command was made illegal by the authorities.

America, land of plenty—what does that say to me? America, land of freedom. America, with its toy soldiers, its beautiful gardens, its sumptuous homes, its hot dogs and ice cream, its deserts and snowfields—what are they to me?

For there dwelt in his breast only his pent-up rage; there was no other emotion.

To play Jun-ho's game, if he himself were to sell off his home, his furniture, and all the other things he had obtained through his blood and sweat, the proceeds would barely amount to a tiny breadstore on a street corner in this huge land of America.

"*Hyeong*! The ocean! The ocean, *Hyeong*!"

And there it was in front of them, like a gigantic barrier. It was as if a curtain had been drawn wide open to reveal the backdrop of a stage. It was all so unexpected.

The water was deep blue, almost black. Rough waves clawed at the bluffs along the shore.

The view was clear and unobstructed. The highway had shrunk to two lanes and beneath them was an endless sweep of carved-out promontories.

Beneath the blazing sun the ocean was a taut, tense line clutching at the sky. The foot of the bluffs gaped with ocher soil and chunks of rock contorted in rage that roared as the wild surf lashed at them.

The strong onshore breeze whistled through the open

windows of the car, carrying the hoarse calls of gulls sweeping aloft. The road they had to travel was like an escape route between the bluffs tumbling to the sea and crimson escarpments excavated from the foot of the hills. Tangled tufts of grass straggled uselessly from the bluffs.

Jun-ho parked at an ocean outlook and produced pipe and marijuana from the glove compartment. He carefully pinched the weed tight so no shred of it would be lost, then pressed it against the thin screen at the bottom of the bowl.

By now he knew Jun-ho's habits. Whenever Jun-ho saw a beautiful vista, out came the pipe.

Was that beautiful vista more dazzling when Jun-ho smoked? Was the scene enhanced? If not, had it become necessary for him to hallucinate in order to ease the bottomless lonesomeness and disappointment he felt in the presence of Mother Nature's spectacles? In bed at night, Jun-ho invariably sucked on the pipe, holding his breath with cheeks puffed out, in order to fall asleep.

Did smoking transmute those vistas into something Jun-ho wanted? Did he smoke because of vestiges of the pain that had stung him during the previous four years? Because he was in America, land of freedom, where people didn't interfere? Because of the pleasure he took in gorging himself on freedom?

Jun-ho lit the pipe and eagerly drank in the smoke. He coughed, his adam's-apple bobbing, but none of the precious smoke escaped. All of it had spread within his lungs.

An acrid odor filled the car. The weed was a mound of glowing crimson brought to life by quick drafts sounding like the dry whistling of a bellows. Jun-ho held his breath to take in as much of the smoke as possible.

His bloodshot eyes bulged and his throat swelled like a snake swallowing its prey. When he could hold his breath no more he erupted in a fit of coughing.

"Look there."

His eyes slowly softened, saw nothing in this world, lusterless eyes that looked at him while seeming to gaze at once both near and far, eyes that seemed lost in a dream.

A smile of rapture spread over his face.

"Look, *Hyeong*. The sky. It's beautiful. Like a rainbow. And the waves. Look at the waves."

Jun-ho giggled idiotically. The incongruous laughter signaled his gradual immersion in ecstasy.

Jun-ho extended the pipe. "Have a toke, *Hyeong*."

He shook his head.

"Come on. It's not going to hurt. Just once. Hey, you're starting to look handsome, *Hyeong*." Jun-ho was giggling constantly now. "Wow, look at those seagulls, look—they're like paper cranes."

Loath to waste any of the weed, Jun-ho sucked in and then his cheeks puffed out. But all that remained was black ash. Jun-ho tapped the pipe bowl empty.

"*Hyeong*, what are we doing here, anyway? I can't figure it out. It's really weird."

Jun-ho rummaged through the plastic bag and began wolfing down slices of bread.

He observed Jun-ho's profile. Jun-ho looked so happy. Like a sleepwalker. And so he felt he shouldn't disturb his reveries, either with words or by shaking him awake.

Let him be! he ordered himself.

Let him have his dreams. Don't interfere.

As he ate, Jun-ho closed his eyes listlessly. Bread crumbs clung to his mouth. He noisily gulped juice.

"Where are we, *Hyeong*? Where do you suppose we are? Where are we sitting right this moment?" he mumbled dreamily.

A few gulls hunkered down on the roof of the car to rest their tired wings. Jun-ho had turned pale. Had he sucked in too much smoke all at once? His face was waxy white, the eyes alone rimmed with red.

They couldn't resume their journey till Jun-ho's mind began to clear. He himself was lost in his own reveries, reveries as profound as Jun-ho's. While speeding along the snowy roads of Yosemite Jun-ho had almost habitually produced his pipe at the dazzling spectacle of the utterly white landscape. And into the pipe went marijuana, until Jun-ho was down to a single pinch. He himself was well aware that Jun-ho smoked intermittently while driving, but to do so on an icy road was madness.

"Relax, *Hyeong*." This was the response to the naked scowl he gave Jun-ho whenever the latter smoked marijuana while driving. Reading his expression, Jun-ho would make a point of grinning broadly to put him at ease. "A hit of this actually makes me drive better. No need to worry."

All the past week Jun-ho had sunk into his reveries, little by little. And true to his words, there was nothing in his driving to find fault with. It did seem, as Jun-ho had said, that a token amount of marijuana was a kind of lubricant, dissolving tension and ridding him of fatigue. Even so, smoking on the sharp, icy curves of Yosemite's sheer roads was just plain senseless. It was suicidal. And so he had snatched the pipe from Jun-ho—only a few puffs were left—and emptied it out the window.

Purple with rage, Jun-ho had torn into him: "What'd you do that for? That was my last hit! I paid those Mexicans sixty bucks—it's all I had left! You're the one who's nuts, *Hyeong*, not me!"

"Listen, you fucking idiot, I don't want to die. I didn't

come on this trip to kill myself," he coldly responded.

"No more beautiful scenery. Fuck! Things just don't come out at me if I don't smoke."

"So, you're going to end up an illegal just so you can smoke away?"

"This isn't heroin, for Christ sake. And it's better for you than booze."

Jun-ho had to resign himself, and all the rest of the way through Yosemite and on to San Francisco he kept a morose silence, like someone who had fallen into a severe depression. All along, he himself had felt apologetic to Jun-ho but hadn't expressed this in words. Perhaps Jun-ho was right—perhaps the innocent-looking weedlike thing was less harmful than booze. Perhaps it was a harmless plant with medicinal properties, a substance that offered comfort through modest hallucinations when one was depressed or suffered pangs of loneliness—or so it seemed to him, who had never tried it. This weed was the only thing that soothed Jun-ho's fears. Why did I take it away from him? What gave me the right to take his source of comfort, his anesthetic? He's a very lonely man, and a little bit is all he needs in order to cope.

Eyes still closed, Jun-ho lurched to his feet. Where the ground dropped off toward the ocean he began retching. The juice and bread he had just eaten came up.

"First time that's ever happened. Must have had too much."

Jun-ho lifted his pale face and looked back at him. Tears had gathered in his eyes.

"Let's go, *Hyeong*. Sorry."

3

Past the Carmel coast they went, past the luxuriant wooded seaside of Big Sur, past Lucia and Gorda. The highway stretched out ahead of them, clinging always to the coast. So little traffic did it carry, it might as well have been a single lane rather than two. On and on they went, but there was only the sea, and from time to time on the left a hilly area or an open pasture. Resort homes, half concealed like bird nests, perched precariously on the seaside bluffs.

After a thousand-plus miles with little respite the car labored like a distance runner but showed no signs of breakdown. They had driven so fast for so long, they sometimes felt as if man and machine had become a single unit. Winding along Route 1, following the sloping bluffs, they reached a state in which no thoughts registered upon their consciousness. While the hands on the steering wheel moved mechanically in response to the curves, turning sometimes slowly, sometimes quickly, the eyes rested on some indistinct curve in the distance—the mind had become a blank slate. This oblivion was a kind of reflex action, a reflex that occurs when self-consciousness is absent.

Conversation dies out—no surprise there. Nor do they bother with music.

A leaden silence settles over them. The passing scenery, the ocean, the sun slanting across the sky, the crimson twilight—eventually they cease to register. All sense of time and space crystallizes.

The car gallops along like a racehorse with blinders, which direct it toward the finish, following a single, infinite line as it unfolds among the network of roads.

Now they're in Cambria, and now Morro Bay. The occasional sports car passes and they try to keep up. But this beater of theirs, worthy though it is, can't catch the sports car, which is built for speed. After staying close for a time it falls back, once again a solitary long-distance runner on a deserted course. It's now afternoon, and oncoming traffic virtually disappears. No more cars come up behind them. Every now and then they spy a vacation house on the bluffs, but it gives them no sense of a human presence.

The seashore is an abandoned waste, like a dump. It's bordered by cities, but they see no young people riding the waves, only the sea clawing at the fringes of this area where land meets ocean.

Deep Blue Night **53**

All that moves are the gulls and the steadfast sun. The sunshine changes frequently, sometimes dazzling, sometimes ecstatic, sometimes offering a drawn and sickly visage. At times a long streamer of clouds obscures it, seems to abduct it. Where are those dark streamers taking the sun, blindfolded and gagged? You don't want to think about it. The wind blows, then dies down—but for how long?

Headlands, ripped and crumpled like aluminum foil, sink into the sea. What was originally a single entity has been rent in two by a wrathful god, land and sea divided by bluffs and cliffs.

No point in looking at the map. Los Angeles remains a long distance away. They drive without stopping, but the road has so many ups and downs they can't go as fast as they want. Doesn't look like they'll reach Los Angeles tonight. But they'll have to keep driving. They can't afford a motel. If not tonight, then they ought to be able to make Los Angeles tomorrow morning.

At any rate they have a destination, and for that they're thankful. But there's no one in Los Angeles to greet them with joy. Just as no one sent them off, no one will welcome them back.

If they'd fallen to their deaths from the rock walls of Yosemite, their bodies wouldn't be discovered till spring. And who would be able to identify them?

Perhaps a page out of their passports would be found. They could have died in Death Valley, or in Yosemite, or on Route 99. But they hadn't. If they'd died in a shattering collision on Route 99, no one could have identified them, no one could have known their destination, no one could have explained why they were on that highway. And the same held true in Los Angeles, their destination now. If they died in their sleep, it would be a month before anyone discovered them. A month before a Mexican in the apartment next door, who didn't know their faces, would be hit by the stench and break down their door. But why think about death? Yes, rage was bottled up inside him like bubbling lava, but he wasn't yet at the age to consider death. It wasn't for the sake of death that he'd left on this trip. It was the rage. But why? Why the rage? What was it that made him so angry? And what was it that made Jun-ho fearful, that made him take up marijuana again? What could have made him abandon his family and become an illegal alien?

The car gradually picks up speed. At Morro Bay, Route 1 briefly leaves the coast and joins U.S. 101. Route 101 is thronged with vehicles that rage like beasts. They roll along like grain falling from a thresher. Listen to the whine they make. Their car is sucked up in the flow. Other cars pass, or come alongside; the occupants are tight-lipped. When their car accelerates it makes a kissing sound as tires meet the expressway surface. There's a faint shudder of the chassis that you can feel through your skin. It's not yet dark, but headlights come on. The cars charge forward in an asphalt jungle, like the beasts that run the African savannas, like a herd of wild animals abandoning an area after one of them, surprised perhaps by a hunter, darts off. The vehicles move furiously, like fleeing giraffes, rhinos, hippos, ostriches, all manner of beasts. Nothing exists but the sensation of speed.

They leave 101, turning again onto Route 1, and an odd loneliness creeps into them. The sun is about to set. The sun god, monarch of day, yields up his throne. The evening glow, betraying the daylight, revolts in a display of crimson banners. The seas are higher. Little by little, headlights grow distinct. The sun finally expires, but its halo holds sway over all. With one final hemorrhage it has dyed the heavens. Dusk gnaws like a mouse at the gate of day. Like an anesthetized patient losing consciousness on the operating table, day finally disappears into the cavern of dusk, gnawing now at an afterglow the faint color of a first menstrual flow. It is sublime, this poignant beauty. The sun has finally disappeared, but the golden light mixing with the evening glow produces a grand display of fireworks. The army of the sea launches a concentrated fusillade against the disintegrating realm of heaven. Shells explode in a burst of sparks, illuminating the darkness on high with shards of light.

The car moves desperately on. The headlights are pillars of light, bright like the eyes of deep-sea fish. The red reflectors lining the highway float like fireflies. Day is gone and blackness is all around. The moon can't be seen. But numerous stars are visible, embedded in the night sky. His field of vision is cut off. The sea, a cunning, crouching predator, is visible only as a darker presence. The bluffs too are invisible—only a flicker of light now and then from the houses perched there. His head clears. His mind is lucid, like water. The car speeds along, a screw drilled into the thick wall of darkness. They go and they go, but with no end in sight to that wall. The headlights grope an inch ahead of the fast-moving car like the feelers of a sightless insect.

Jun-ho grips the wheel silently. He hasn't said a word all afternoon. And with he himself it's the same. They sit together, fixed in absolute solitude. The car rolls along by itself like a globe rotating freely. Roadsigns lit by the headlights rise up like soldiers on night watch, nameless meteors greeting the car as it skims through limitless space. A sign appears—"Grover City"—and quickly recedes. The speedometer reads seventy. The needle climbs higher, then it drops lower, up and down, shuddering at an unattainable crossroads. The fuel gauge barely registers. They'll need to fill up to get to Los Angeles. If they run out of gas on this desolate stretch of highway in the middle of the night, they're helpless. But now it's a bother to talk. Maybe a town will show up before they run out; maybe there's forty miles on what they've got left. And if they do run out they can urinate into the tank. The urine will bring up another ten miles' worth of gas.

The car seems to stop in place, and it's the highway that flows by. They feel like miners extending a mine shaft. From the far end of the highway come the quivering headlights of onrushing cars. The lights become ever clearer as they approach. And then for a brief instant faces meet and skim past, and the disappearing vehicle, like a boy with a flashlight wandering a field, retraces the route he and Jun-ho have taken. Jun-ho occasionally releases the wheel and shakes a numb or aching hand. The ocean is unseen, but the foamy waves beating against the rocks glint like psychedelic lights on a dancer's tights. The waves smack their lips together. The center stripe clings to the highway as it runs madly along ahead of the car. It's like the sharpened blade of a fodder chopper, and the car is a shaman dancing barefoot on the blue steel of its edge. The car, its furious speed palpable, quivers like an animal on the point of ejaculation. With each turn in the twisting road, the wheels screech and spark, like a dull knife whetted on a grindstone. As the speed increases, the darkness falls behind. The speedometer reads eighty. A dangerous speed. But he doesn't care to open his mouth to caution Jun-ho. Leave him alone, he decides.

The car rounds a curve on the overhanging road and immediately slows down, wailing in agony. They've eaten nothing all afternoon, but they have no appetite. Their stomachs feel empty, but it's worth putting up with. Chewing dried-out slices of bread is like chewing sand. They don't consider spreading out the map to see where they are. To see the map they'd need the interior light. And that would mean seeing each other's face. Depressing it would be to see each other's gloomy aspect in the light. Let it be, he decides. If they continue on Route 1 they'll make it. That's all. Clearly they're past the halfway point of their long journey. Maybe farther. Perhaps they'll reach Los Angeles in a very short time. But no. It's only wishful thinking. It may be that they'll never arrive. Perhaps they're racing along blindly in search of an illusory city in a nonexistent world. Los Angeles is a fictitious place name; it doesn't exist in this world. They've been speeding thousands of miles toward this fictitious city. But no matter. No need to try to divine what's there at the end of Route 1. There's one thing that's clear: they're certainly alive because they can feel the speed. Through the windshield they glimpse the outline of an animal leaping frantically through the oncoming headlights then taking cover in the darkness.

A dog that's lost its way home? A coyote separated from the pack?

Scattered clumps of dirt are visible on the roadside where they've tumbled from the heights. But nowhere is a human form to be seen. Fallen branches from the dense brush lie on the road like so many bones stripped of flesh. The sky has a lucid clarity, the clarity not of moonlight but of countless stars shining in unison like multicolored Christmas lights. Among them are stars newly formed whose light has only now arrived across hundreds of millions of light-years of space, as well as stars that have just expired. Shooting stars track thickly across the sky, perhaps collapsing under their own weight.

And then—

Jun-ho, who hasn't said a word, opens the glove compartment and produces a cassette. He slides it into the tape player and switches it on. He himself knows all too well what it is—a tape sent by Jun-ho's wife. They've listened to it dozens of times during their trip—so frequently that he could memorize its thirty minutes from beginning to end.

The tape slowly unwinds and the voice of Jun-ho's wife issues from the speakers:

"It's been a while. I received your letter. As you requested, I'm getting the children ready to say something.... (pause) How have you been? I spend all my time looking after the children. At least you're healthy, and that's a relief, but what I worry about most is how you're eating, sleeping, whether you have enough clothes.... I know your lazy personality all too well, and I'm always afraid you're going to turn into a beggar, the way you go around in any old clothes until they start to smell, going a week or more not washing your face, not brushing your teeth. And you need to wash your feet every other day at least. Same thing with shampooing. And for heaven's sake don't grow that mustache.... (pause) I don't know quite what to say. We've never really had a nice talk face to face, you and I, and it feels kind of awkward and strange to talk into a tape recorder as if I'm looking at you.... (pause) There were some articles about you in the weekly magazines and such, saying you've settled in the U.S. They were kind of sarcastic, but now they've quieted down.... (pause) Lately Jun-gyeom's been asking for you. Dozens of times a day he asks where Daddy went. I tell him Daddy went to the U.S. He thinks you hopped on a robot and went to meet an alien from space. He thinks the U.S. is

Andromeda, the constellation in that cartoon show. Believes you've left for outer space on one of those Marzingers to drive off aliens who are invading Earth.... Eun-gyeong's going into second grade. She doesn't ask about you as much as Jun-gyeom. She's starting to grow up, and she keeps it all inside—a few days ago I saw a page of the diary she's supposed to hand in at school, and it was all about you.... (pause) She wondered why Daddy didn't come home, thought it was strange. She asked God to make you come back.... (telephone rings) It's the telephone—I'll be right back.... (pause) Okay, we can talk some more. Where was I?... (pause) Jun-gyeom! Jun-gyeom, come and say hi to Daddy.... (pause) Where's Daddy? No Daddy here. Daddy's in the tape player, stupid. Don't lie, Sister, Daddy didn't go into that little tape player. Sister's a liar.... (from the background) Say hi to Daddy.... (from up close) Daddy, I'm Jun-gyeom. Where are you, Daddy? You're on a Marzinger beating up bad aliens. When are you coming? I wanna ride the robot too, Daddy. I'm gonna be a spaceman when I grow up. Those bad space people, they invade green planet Earth, I'll beat 'em up.... Daddy, I'm bored.... Mommy's crying sometimes.... (recorder clicks off; pause; from the background) Jun-gyeom, how about a song for Daddy? No! Just one song for Daddy—good boy. Where's Daddy? I won't sing unless Daddy's here.... There's our Jun-gyeom—good boy.... Now stand up.... Sing a song (pause; abruptly and forcefully) '*Ooo, ttadada, ooo, ttadada, brave warriors of justice, flying fast as lightning, who would there be without us? Ooo, ttadada, ooo, ttadada, they're coming, don't be afraid, and crush 'em, warriors of justice flying on Marzingers, ooo, ttadada, ooo, ttadada....*' (clapping; from the background) Bravo! All right, Eun-gyeong, your turn. Eun-gyeong's lost all her front teeth. '*Mice without their front teeth shouldn't go near the well.*'... (pause) Daddy.... (pause) Daddy.... (pause; singing) '*The rose moss is blooming, the balsam is blooming, in the garden Daddy and I made. And the morning glory's blooming, as nice as the others, follows the trail strung up by Daddy....*' (clapping) Now, the two of you together. Stand up nice and straight, then bow to Daddy.... (pause) '*The peach trees, the pear trees, the baby azaleas are abloom in the valleys of my old hometown. I long for the times when I played in my village as the colorful royal palace of flowers took form....*' (clapping; pause) Don't know what else there is to say. It's bitterly cold here. Everybody's saying it's the coldest in decades. Apartment buildings have heat but we still need a kerosene stove.... I wish I knew what you.... (long silence) I don't know what you'll.... I wish I knew what you want me to do, I wish you had a plan for us—"

Jun-ho switched off the tape. A heavy silence settled over the interior of the car. He himself, having heard the tape those dozens of times, could recall almost all of what followed from Jun-ho's wife.

With the listless monotone from the tape cut off, the engine sounded that much louder, wheezing like someone with a bad cough as the car sped through the night. And then it was screaming, unable to hold up longer, driven without respite. The chassis began to shake violently. There was a sound—was something coming apart? The taciturn, uncomplaining car had grown hot, a mass of metal subject to constant heat, and it shook as if reaching its breaking point.

The temperature light was on—the car had overheated. A danger signal. The car seethed like boiling water. It had reached its limit and could take no more.

But Jun-ho didn't slow down. Didn't ease up although they'd be in trouble if he didn't turn off the engine and give it a long rest to cool down. Instead he accelerated.

The speedometer needle passed seventy-five, closed in on eighty.

The car shuddered, a mute appeal for release from pain. The needle crept toward eighty-five. The chassis trembled like the hand of an alcoholic going through withdrawal, and the car flew down the narrow highway. It lurched along the solid center line at a frenzied pace, as if it would plunge to earth. It was like an airplane rolling down the runway for takeoff.

Danger signals bore into his brain. Yet he kept his mouth shut.

Leave him alone, he commanded himself. Leave him alone. Let him do what he wants.

Suddenly there was a burning smell. Thick clouds of smoke issued from the hood and enveloped the car. Vision became hazy. The car left the road and skidded toward the guard rail at an overlook. With a sharp bang the front of the car met the solid iron railing. The car barely stopped. Any faster, and the impact would have broken the guard rail and the car would have plunged over the bluff. One of the headlights had shattered against the barrier. The two of them were absolutely still, as if senseless. Smoke streamed from the hood. If they didn't quickly top off the radiator with water, the overheated engine would catch fire and burn up.

But Jun-ho remained motionless, hands on the wheel. He himself studied Jun-ho in profile. He couldn't believe what he saw: Jun-ho was weeping. The remaining headlight faintly illuminated the interior of the car, and the tears rolling down Jun-ho's face.

"I'm going," Jun-ho mumbled in a sodden voice. "I'm going back. Going to book me a seat on an airplane the minute we get to Los Angeles. Got a round-trip ticket when I came over here, so no problem. I'm going back, *Hyeong*. I've made up my mind."

With the back of his hand Jun-ho kept wiping away the tears flowing down his cheeks.

"What are we doing sitting here? This country's not for us. Why are we here? Tell me the reason. I can't get anything here, can't find anything."

He listened in silence to Jun-ho's sobbing words. Jun-ho wiped violently at his face, abashed at his display of tears.

"How much fucking farther do we have to go?" Jun-ho's voice was deliberately sullen. "We still got a long way."

"Yes, still a long way. Probably early tomorrow morning before we get there."

"We've gone four thousand miles, no rest stop, and we still got a long way. What's the deal? We've gone as far as we could. We had to take Route One. But I get the feeling we're way off track.—Hey, look! You're crazy, *Hyeong*! Can't even read a map, you loony bastard! You're out of your mind! Look there!"

Jun-ho cut the headlight, then turned it on again. Beside the guard rail was a road sign. The light illuminated the number of the highway they'd been following: 246 West.

"Look! What's going on? We've been on Two Forty-six. What happened to One? Where did it disappear to? I told you we had to take One south. That's how we get to Los Angeles. Will you please look at the map. Don't just sit there."

Jun-ho turned on the interior light. He himself ripped open the road atlas.

"Whereabouts are we? Tell me. I don't see Route One. What's the story? For all I know we're on our way to Alaska. Shit!"

Jun-ho banged on the steering wheel in exasperation. The horn put out a faint sound.

He himself, sitting quietly until then, suddenly chuckled. A foamy smile spread over his face.

"The map's wrong. We've been fooled. The map got us off track."

"Are you serious? No way. We were on our way to Los Angeles, that's for sure. If we go back the way we came, we'll hit Route One. We got off the main drag by mistake, that's all."

"We'll never get to Los Angeles," he said, still chuckling. "I know what's going on. Route One's never gone to Los Angeles. Or Route Two or Route Three for that matter. They'd never get us to Los Angeles. You see, there's no such city as Los Angeles. It's all in the imagination, a name on a map. Try going back the way we came—you'll never meet up with One."

"I'm going. I'm going back."

Jun-ho tried to start the car. Nothing happened. The car had cooled to a chill, but was now immobile. Jun-ho feverishly turned the ignition switch. No reaction. He pumped the gas pedal and released the ignition, with as much effect as a lifeguard giving artificial respiration to a drowning victim.

"Engine's shot. Or else we're out of gas. Anyway, we're not going anywhere—car's dead. Have to wait till it's light."

"You talk like you hoped this would happen. Well, I can make it. I can get this car going. I know this car better than anybody. The headlight coming on proves the engine's not completely shot. The car's fine—it's tired, that's all."

Jun-ho gave the steering wheel a desperate jerk. His face was a mass of sweat mixed with tears.

"If we stay put we're dead. Late at night the temperature goes down. We don't start the car, we don't get heat. We freeze to death. We're out in the middle of nowhere. Maybe nobody around for dozens of miles. Maybe all sorts of animals waiting to jump us. What do you think? You listening? Say something."

Instead of answering he opened the glove compartment, produced the pipe and the handful of marijuana that remained, and offered it to Jun-ho. Jun-ho looked at him in wonderment.

"Don't be scared. Light up. Then you'll be happy. You can sleep. You can dream. We won't die, not a chance of it. See that black stuff moving around out there? Know what that is? It's the ocean. The Pacific Ocean. Goes all the way to the country you're going back to. We'll get back, I'm sure of it. We'll find our way. When it's daylight, we'll get back. Los Angeles isn't far. We'll catch a plane there and in no time we'll be flying over that ocean."

"*Hyeong*!" Jun-ho's voice was tense. "What the hell are you doing?"

"If you don't want it, I'll smoke it myself."

As he had always seen Jun-ho do, he took some of the weed between his fingertips, crushed it into a tiny ball, and packed it against the thin screen in the pipe bowl.

"That's more than you need. Don't be stupid. This stuff's potent. Too potent for someone like you who's smoking for the first time."

He found matches, lit up, drew in deeply. Immediately the pieces of dried plant glowed crimson. The smoke filled his mouth and he took it deep into his lungs. His chest pounded as if it would burst. He sensed a coughing fit but contained it, like someone trying to hold his breath underwater longer than anyone else, and waited for the smoke to permeate the far reaches of his lungs. His eyeballs bulged as if to pop out. He was overdoing it. He tried, and failed, to stifle a cough.

As he sucked in smoke again he clutched at his head. He felt as if the smoke was seeping into every part of his brain. Smoke from the potent plant settled over him, as if his head were a piece of meat being smoke-cured.

Suddenly he was very dizzy. He lost his balance and his head lurched against the window. Then he managed to straighten himself. His eyes, shining like an animal's, seemed never to have been more keen. He felt a searing, wrenching pressure in his chest. He struggled against this feeling of suffocation, as if resisting someone who was strangling him. He inhaled, but now there was no pressure. It was as if his airways had burst. Something leaked out of him and floated away. He was completely drained of energy.

From somewhere in the far distance he heard a faint voice.

"*Hyeong*, are you all right? Tell me honestly."

He saw where the voice had floated in from. The bewildered expression he saw there was contorting into a monstrous shape, like a vegetable undergoing a mutation.

"I'm fine," he replied confidently. He had the strange feeling that it was not he himself who had spoken but someone else, someone who had borrowed his mouth.

Slowly he sat up. He opened the door and stumbled out.

"*Hyeong*, where are you going?"

"To get some air."

"Uh-uh. It's dangerous. Stay here. Come on back. Uh-uh. Please. What the hell are you doing?"

He bumped against the guard rail and glared toward the foot of the bluff. The wind stormed like the madly swirling mane of a horse. The crashing of the surf came toward him like the footsteps of an army that didn't know retreat. Booms reverberated from somewhere, like the beating of a large drum.

The bluff wasn't steep. It was only a small headland whose base fell steeply toward the sea. A path stretched out, and down it he bounded.

He stumbled and fell but rose immediately. Down the path he went, bounding, running, falling. His tottering steps came to a stop against the pebbles heaped on the beach. The shore contained more stones than he could ever hope to count.

There was no moonlight, but the gathered light of the luxuriant stars, shining in unison, were alms for his eyes, brightening them, and he could see whatever he wanted.

Spray from the fierce waves rained down on him, soaking him. He knelt in a heap on the pebbles. He felt happiness, pleasure, sadness.

He sprawled out on the stones, like a corpse washed

across the sea by the rough waves. Those waves, which had banished him to an alien land, swiftly retreated, and those just arrived, carrying nothing, netted him.

And then, finally, he saw the embers of his seething rage slowly die out. It wasn't that his wave-borne exile to alien shores had put his rage to sleep. Rather, he felt as if his entire life, all he had ever seen and heard, the honor and empty fame he had possessed and wasted, the law and justice he had believed to be right, the ambitions sometimes realized and sometimes betrayed, the pleasures and sexual appetite he had pursued without end, the plentiful supply of women he had possessed for a time and discarded, all these things that had beaten him mercilessly had finally and awfully conquered him. And when he realized he had been conquered, his rage was truly reduced to ashes.

Now there was no reason for spite, loathing, animosity, hatred, and all the rest. Kissing the surface of the hard rocks, he begged forgiveness of all the conquerors who had made him submit. Surely, he pledged to himself, it was time to return. Utterly exhausted, he wanted comfort from someone, anyone.

The Poplar Tree

He was an unusual man.

For a time he was a high-jumper. At his best he routinely cleared 2.3 meters. He was more than a match for anyone in the village.

His personal best was 2.4 meters. No matter how tall you were, he could leap over you. As he could any wall, without ruffling a shirtsleeve—he made it look effortless. He was a splendid man, the sort you rarely see.

It was only a matter of time until he set a new world record, everyone thought at one point. But he wasn't a professional athlete. He was a blacksmith, a maker of sickles, axes, and such.

People liked to watch him high-jump.

We used to ask him to jump for us. But since he wasn't a professional, we didn't make a high-jump bar for him, the kind that wobbles and falls if you brush it on the way over, and we didn't prepare a sand pit to soften his landing. Instead we'd ask him to jump over a tall bush clover fence, or else a couple of the tallest of us kids would make like a horse and rider and dare him to jump over our heads.

He didn't often give in to a straightforward request to jump. At the same time, he didn't want people to think his talent for high-jumping had gone to his head, so if we phrased our request in the form of a dare it always worked. He'd strip to the waist, crouch down before the object to be jumped, and then, whoosh, he was a mad whirl of motion, riding on the wind, slicing clean over whoever stood on the "horse." Not once did he fall short. Quite a man, he was.

And because we thought him quite a man, we convinced ourselves that one day he would clear the flagpole at the school playground.

As for me, I believed he would one day jump a great mountain at a single bound. At a single bound he would clear the clouds floating in the sky, grab the stars that twinkled beyond, and drop them at our feet. And if only he wanted, at a single bound he would clear not only the crimson twilight painting a distant peak but the rainbow that follows a shower in the western sky, the rainbow resplendent as the striped sleeves of a girl's *saekdong* jacket.

"Uncle, can you jump over that rainbow?"

"Of course I can," he confidently replied. "As long as I have a runway that stretches out nice and wide all the way to the horizon."

But he couldn't jump higher than 2.4 meters. That was as far up as he went. It was also the height of the highest chinup bar at our school playground. There wasn't one of us who could even reach that bar from the ground.

Great as he was, though, he was not a happy man. One summer all three of his children drowned while playing in a stream, first one going under and then the older ones lost in their turn while attempting a rescue. The news drove his wife mad, and eventually she disappeared. And then the peddler of women's items who came around to the village once a month reported having seen her—once at the seashore, once beside a grave, and some time or other at the riverside. And to us she reported that the woman had sprouted scales all over—but not a word of it did we believe.

After losing his children and wife the man turned a bit strange. He still made horseshoes, sickles, and hammers, but his sickles couldn't cut grass and his hammers couldn't drive a nail. He didn't high-jump. People mocked him: he couldn't even clear a brook that us children could jump across.

It got to the point where he'd spend all day in his shop working the bellows but never producing anything, not even a horseshoe.

He was crazy, all the villagers scoffed, but we remained true to him as always—he was our hero. I continued to believe he could jump the flagpole if only he wanted, continued to believe he would one day clear the lovely colors of the rainbow unscathed. Whenever the opportunity presented itself, we asked him to jump over the highest chinup bar for us. But he would shake his head.

"Little ones, I can't jump high anymore—my legs are rusty."

But we didn't believe him. You see, he was our hope.

"Yes you can, Uncle. You can jump over it. You're a great man."

Finally, not wanting to disappoint us, he gave in. A mad dash down the playground, and he soared into the air. But his jump was ridiculously short. His leg hooked the bar and he fell to the ground with a scream, breaking the limb.

His leg was never the same again. He hobbled when he walked. He couldn't jump thirty centimeters high. A frog could have outjumped him. He couldn't even hop from one stepping stone to the next across the stream—you could bet he would fall in.

One day he planted a poplar sapling in his yard. I helped him. But why was he doing this? The reason escaped me. He'd planted tomatoes and Chinese cabbages, peppers and squashes there, and had lived a hand-to-mouth existence on these foods. So the idea of planting a poplar tree instead of a fruit tree whose produce he could readily consume was incomprehensible.

Finally I asked him.

"Because a poplar grows tall faster than any other tree."

"But...a poplar doesn't produce any fruit, Uncle. Why not plant an apple tree or a peach tree?"

"No, little one," he said with a smile. "I don't go hungry anymore. I've got all the tomatoes and potatoes I want."

"Then what are you planting a poplar for?"

"So I can jump higher."

And with that he hobbled to the freshly planted tree and jumped over the single shoot.

"See, I jumped over that tree—I jumped it."

"But Uncle, I can jump over it, too."

So saying, I proudly demonstrated.

"But every day that tree will grow a little taller. A year from now it'll be as tall as you are. In two years it'll be as tall as that chinup bar, in three years it'll be up to the flagpole, in four years up to the electric pole, and in five years it'll grow to the sky. Every day I'm going to jump over that tree. If I can keep it up, then one day I'll be able to jump as high as the sky."

Every day he watered the tree; every day he put his heart into making it grow. True to his word, the tree did grow, but it wasn't noticeably larger every morning like, say, a morning glory, which seems to spurt up overnight when it blooms. Its growth seemed retarded—just like the hour hand of a clock, which doesn't appear to move at all.

And every day he jumped over the tree, hobble and all.

A year later, the poplar tree was as tall as I. Its verdant leaves trembled in the wind like the bracken-fern hands of schoolchildren cheering on the playground.

"Look," he said proudly. "I'm jumping over the tree."

And right before my eyes he half ran, half hobbled up to the poplar and cleared it.

Before we knew it we were growing too. Some of us were already sneaking cigarettes out in the wheat fields and no longer paid him much attention. We were gradually learning new pleasures, finding more interesting things to do. Along with our curiosity about pleasures we'd never tasted—alcohol, tobacco, girls, and such—black hair was growing by the day in our nether regions.

I alone continued to visit him, and it was for me alone that he half hobbled, half ran to the poplar tree and jumped over it.

After two years the poplar had outgrown me and was tall as the lower chinup bar. At the time, I was in love with a girl. Her beauty dazzled me, and on the low dikes among the rice paddies she would whisper to me.

"I don't love you, and I don't want you. There's nobody I like except him." She indicated a scarecrow standing amid the golden ears of rice. "I'm going to marry him. I'm going to have his baby."

Poking out of the rice paddies in autumn were countless scarecrows, each one a trunk of straw beneath a tattered farmer's hat. The flocks of sparrows weren't the least bit daunted. It was beyond me why the girl had said she loved a scarecrow.

For several days I went alone to the rice paddies and stood with my arms out like a scarecrow. And on one of those days I saw the girl and a man take off their clothes and roll around among the drooping stalks of rice. The girl then carried the child of the man, and not the scarecrow. The girl was a liar.

After I'd gotten over my sorrow, I went to see the blacksmith.

"Now just you watch, I'm going to jump over that tree," he proclaimed. "I can do it."

He hobbled up to the tree and cleared it.

"What'd I tell you? I'll jump over that tree as high as it grows. Yes I will."

But he was older now and bent-over. An old man, really, and that was the extent of it. All but two of his teeth were gone. His three children had long since perished, and his wife still hadn't returned.

"I saw his wife," the peddler of women's things reported. "She makes rice cakes out of sand at the seashore and sells them at the market. I tried one—scrumptious! 'Your husband's waiting for you,' I told her. 'Why not go back with me?' And this is what she said—'You tell him he can wait. He can wait till I've made rice cakes out of all that sand and sold every last one of them.'"

After three years the poplar was tall as the flagpole. It was a very handsome tree. Its roots were planted firmly in the ground and the vibrant young limbs stretched out wide as you please. Its leaves were as lush as the hair growing from a man's broad chest. Compared with the tree, the blacksmith was an old man approaching death. The mouth that spoke to me now held only one tooth.

"Good to see you, little one. Watch close, because I'm going to jump over that tree."

He still called me "little one." Unfortunately I was no longer a little one—I was a young man.

He started running, a slow-motion hobble. And then he was up like the wind, a bird in flight, gently brushing the air like the needles of a silver fir. Over the poplar he went.

"There, you saw it! I jumped it! I jumped that poplar tree!"

After four years the poplar had grown to the sky. You should have seen it—the top was no longer visible. Birds built nests of twigs and straw in its branches and laid their eggs. Low-lying clouds draped the midsection of the tree. In summer the whole village turned out to nap at the foot of the poplar; there was so much shade, you didn't have to fight for it.

"I saw the blacksmith's wife up above the clouds. She lives in a shelter she made on the top branches. She has three children. Honest. If you don't believe me, climb up there and see for yourself."

So said one of the more mischievous youngsters after climbing the tree all the way above the clouds.

Of course, since I wasn't a little boy anymore, I didn't have the lightness of body to climb the tree and see whether things above the clouds were as this boy had said.

When next I saw the blacksmith he had aged completely. His one remaining tooth was gone.

"Well, well, little one," he said with a smile of

delight. "From the time you were young you asked if I could jump over the clouds—remember?"

"Indeed I do, Grandfather."

"Well, here's your chance. I want you to watch me jump over that tree."

He made a long approach, hobbling as best he could. Then suddenly he was aloft, sucked into the sky. I gazed reverently toward the top of the tree he had soared over. He couldn't be seen. I waited for him to return to earth. But he never came down. At first I thought it was because the poplar was so high—high enough that its top couldn't be spotted. So I waited till the sun set, but still he didn't land. And then after the longest time something fell to the ground with a thunk. I picked it up—a wornout shoe.

Recently I visited the village. Brought the wife and our two children. The village had changed, but the poplar still stood. Strange thing was, it now looked very small to me, stunted even. Its leaves were withered, its branches broken. It was painfully contorted, like the body of a drowning victim.

When would he reappear before our eyes, landing on the ground, the form of this unusual man who had jumped higher than anyone on earth?

This morning I'm going to plant an apple tree in our yard, a tree that grows very, very slowly. Every morning

I'll jump over that tree. And one day I'll jump over the clouds and at long last meet up with him in that other world, that unusual place he disappeared to.

You see, I've finally learned. Learned that the world we live in is actually a stopping point, a place to which we leaped from the distant place we once inhabited; that we'll move on to an earth that will receive our tired souls for all time. Yes, we are hanging in the balance, all of us. We are all going around upside down.

About the author

Choe In-ho (b. 1945) is one of the prodigies of modern Korean fiction, a literate, widely read man who has been a professional writer all his working life. He published his first story at the age of eighteen, graduated from Yonsei University with a degree in English literature, and since the 1970s has devoted much of his creative energy to the novel. With his contemporary Kim Seung-ok he deserves credit for charging Korean fiction of the late 1960s and beyond with a fluid, visual style (he is also a screenwriter), a rich imagination, and a keen wit. *Deep Blue Night* was first published in 1982 in the journal *Munye Jung-ang* and was honored with that year's Yi Sang Literature Award. *The Poplar Tree* first appeared in 1981 in the journal *Munhak Sasang*.

About the translators

Bruce and Ju-Chan Fulton are the translators of several anthologies of modern Korean fiction. Bruce Fulton was recently appointed Young Bin Min Professor of Korean Literature and Literary Translation at the University of British Columbia. The Fultons live in Seattle.

The Portable Library of Korean Literature

Short Fiction · 1
The Wings Yi Sang | Trans. Ahn Jung-hyo & James B. Lee

Short Fiction · 2
A Dwarf Launches a Little Ball Cho Se-hui | Trans. Chun Kyung-Ja

Short Fiction · 3
The Cry of the Magpies Kim Dong-ni | Trans. Sol Soonbong

Short Fiction · 4
The Wounded Yi Chongjun | Trans. Jennifer M. Lee

Short Fiction · 5
Deep Blue Night Choe In-ho | Trans. Bruce and Ju-Chan Fulton

Short Fiction · 6
The Ma Rok Biographies Seo Giwon | Trans. Kevin O'Rourke

Short Fiction · 7
The Land of the Banished Cho Chong-Rae | Trans. Chun Kyung-Ja

Short Fiction · 8
Three Days in That Autumn Pak Wanseo | Trans. Ryu Sukhee

Short Fiction · 9
The Rainy Spell Yun Heung-gil | Trans. Suh Ji-moon

Short Fiction · 10
The Other Side of Dark Remembrance
Lee Kyun-young | Trans. Ahn Jung-hyo

Short Fiction · 11
With Her Oil Lamp On, That Night
Lim Chul-Woo | Trans. Agnita M. Tennant & Ahn Jung-hyo

Short Fiction · 12
Between Heaven and Earth Yun Daenyeong | Trans. Kim Sul Ja